Colors

Los colores

lohs koh-*loh*-rehs

Illustrated by Clare Beaton

Ilustraciones de Clare Beaton

BARRON'S

green

verde

vehr-deh

white

blanco, blanca

blahn-koh, *blahn*-kah

red

rojo, roja

roh-hoh, *roh*-hah

black

negro, negra

neh-groh, *neh*-grah

pink

rosa

roh-sah

blue

azul

ah-sool

orange

naranja

nah-*rahn*-hah

gray

gris

grees

yellow

amarillo, amarilla

ah-mah-*ree*-yoh, ah-mah-*ree*-yah

brown

marrón

mahr-rohn

purple

morado, morada

moh-*rah*-doh, moh-*rah*-dah

A simple guide to pronouncing Spanish words

• Read this guide as naturally as possible, as if it were English.
• Put stress on the letters in *italics*, for example, *roh* in *roh*-sah.

Los colores	lohs koh-*loh*-res	**Colors**
verde	*vehr*-deh	**green**
blanco, blanca	*blahn*-koh, *blahn*-kah	**white**
rojo, roja	*roh*-hoh, *roh*-hah	**red**
negro, negra	*neh*-groh, *neh*-grah	**black**
rosa	*roh*-sah	**pink**
azul	ah-*sool*	**blue**
naranja	nah-*rahn*-hah	**orange**
gris	grees	**gray**
amarillo, amarilla	ah-mah-*ree*-yoh, ah-mah-*ree*-yah	**yellow**
marrón	mahr-*rohn*	**brown**
morado, morada	moh-*rah*-doh, moh-*rah*-dah	**purple**